THE FEAST DAY

by Edwin Fadiman Jr.

The Feast Day

Illustrated by Charles Mikolaycak

Little, Brown and Company/Boston/Toronto

FIRST EDITION

T 03/73

Library of Congress Cataloging in Publication Data

Fadiman, Edwin.
  The feast day.

  SUMMARY: Describes the events of the Feast Day on
which twelve-year-old Joan of Arc receives the vision
which influences the course of her life.
  Bibliography: p.
  1. Jeanne d'Arc, Saint, 1412-1431--Juvenile
literature. [1. Jeanne d'Arc, Saint, 1412-1431.
2. Saints] I. Mikolaycak, Charles, illus.
II. Title.
DC103.5.F3   248'.22'0924 [92]   74-182256
ISBN 0-316-27300-7

Published simultaneously in Canada
by Little, Brown & Company (Canada) Limited

PRINTED IN THE UNITED STATES OF AMERICA

THE FEAST DAY

Everyone knows all good stories begin at the beginning and go on until the end. This story is different. It goes on for just one day. One unbelievable Feast Day.

First, close your eyes and imagine yourself in France (across the Atlantic Ocean) in one special place, called the valley of the Meuse. The valley is not large, though protected by friendly old mountains. In winter, the snow creates fantastic laces in the boughs of the ancient trees and lies like a white furry blanket on the ground.

The valley is even more lovely in summer. And it is summer when our story begins — a story about a girl with black, wide eyes and a warm smile. Her name was Joan.

Joan lived with her family in the village of Domrémy in the year 1425. Joan's home was the house of her father, Jacques d'Arc. It was Jacques who spoke for his people to the great lord, Robert de Baudricourt, when he deigned to come visiting. The village of Domrémy was in fief to Lord Robert, a bluff, red-faced man of middle age, not unkind and not bright. He owned the village and everything in it. Everyone paid taxes to Robert de Baudricourt once a year. The taxes were paid not in money but in things. Hay, chickens, leather — a part of what the village produced went to the lord who owned it.

Jacques d'Arc collected these taxes for Lord Robert and he was a wise and intelligent leader. The people of Domrémy had chosen him to represent them many years ago because he could read and write a little, something Lord Robert could not do.

Jacques had a wife, Isabelle, and three children: two boys and a girl. The youngest was Joan. She was just twelve years old, and today, a bright sunny day in May, was her Feast Day. It was like a second birthday.

Joan had been born in January, but her Feast Day was in May. It was then that she received her presents. It was on this day that everyone wished her luck. She had chosen it herself, with her mother.

Now, early in the morning, she was fast asleep on her sack-bed in the attic of her house. There was only one real bed, and it belonged to her father and mother. Joan and her brothers slept near the open door in full summer, and as close to the fire as they could get during the winter.

Since today was her Feast Day, she had pleaded with her mother to let her best friend, Hauviette, stay with her overnight. The girls had giggled together until much too late.

Now, the sun flooded the attic window, and bathed Joan and her friend in a pearly, white light. The window was made of isinglass — thin shards of a transparent stone that turned the light quite white, the whiteness of a fine pearl.

Hauviette, who was soft and pale — and perhaps just a little fat — opened her eyes, blinked twice, and nudged Joan with her feet.

"It is morning," she said in a sleepy voice. "I'm hungry."

Joan awoke instantly. Before she even opened her eyes, she was smiling to herself. Today would be such a pleasant day. There would be presents. She knew there would. For some time she had noticed her older brother, Jean, working on something in the corner of the large downstairs room, where the family lived and ate. Whenever she tried to approach him to find out what he was doing, he covered his work with his body and told her to go away.

It could mean only one thing. Jean was making a present for her Feast Day.

What would it be, Joan asked herself as she slipped into her shapeless dress and descended the worn rungs of the wooden ladder that led from the attic to the main floor. Hauviette followed her. What had Jean thought up for her Feast Day? He was clever with his hands, he knew what she liked, and she was his favorite. Pierre, the younger boy, was too involved in himself to think much about her. Her father was above such things as small girls' feast days.

As for her mother—Isabelle would give her a present, but it would not be a thing. It is difficult to realize how few things there were then. There were no factories to make them, and no money with which to buy them. Each family was a factory in itself—a small factory creating its own clothes, its own food, its own unhappiness and happiness, too.

Perhaps Jean was making her a doll. Hauviette had a doll, though she no longer played with her. She had been made from leather scraps, and she had had tiny, black stones for eyes. Joan had envied her friend her toy for quite a long time.

The two girls entered the room. The stock-pot bubbled on the iron chain that hung over the small, wood fire. The flames winked in the gray light of the room. There were no windows here.

Isabelle's wedding chest had already been pushed to the center of the room and a board laid upon it. This was the family's dining table. There were three stools. Jean had made them. With his knife he had whittled each of their three legs into a rough, round shape. Then, using fine sand, he had smoothed the wood. The tops were of chestnut—over an inch thick. They had been cut out with an iron saw and were worn and shiny with use.

Joan's mother and father and her elder brother used the stools. When someone came to visit, bringing a cheese or some fruit as his guest gift, then, of course, Joan's brother gave up his stool to the guest. The others ate squatting, Indian fashion.

Joan's nose twitched as she caught the smell of the pot-au-feu. Hauviette said again, "Oh, I'm so hungry."

There were all sorts of good things in this soup. Vegetables in season, meat, even fish, fresh-caught. One of the signs of Jacques d'Arc's prosperity and generosity was that the pot was always full, always ready for a hungry mouth.

"Girls," Isabelle d'Arc said, "go to the well and wash. Then come back quickly for your breakfast."

She was stirring the soup as she spoke. Joan thought, Is she going to wish me a happy Feast Day? Or has she forgotten? But her mother had never forgotten before, and there was no reason for her to begin now. Besides, she knew about Jean's present.

Joan looked at the corner of the room. The small place where Jean had been working was swept clean. It was as though whatever it was was now finished and the cleaning up had just been done. Probably early this morning.

Joan lifted the rope latch of the door. The two girls raced down the small dirt path towards the center of Domrémy and the dark, sweet-smelling well.

Their feet were naked. No one wore shoes in the spring or summer; they were too expensive for everyday use. Like all her friends' Joan's feet had become callused. She could run easily over small, sharp rocks (or snow and ice in the winter, her shoes dangling from her neck by a thick string), and she would feel neither pain nor cold.

The two drew a bucket of water from the well and tipped it into a large, rough wooden bowl they had brought with them. They stared into the water, catching a glimpse of their own faces in the swirling, sun-colored liquid. Joan was always curious to see what she looked like. There were no mirrors, and the well was the only way she could catch a glimpse of herself.

They splashed water over their faces, ran their fingers through their hair, tipped the water out of the bowl, and ran back to the house. The wind of their running dried their wet faces. The sun, just beginning to turn the day to gold, helped too.

It would be a perfect spring day. Warm, but not hot. Joan could smell all the scents of her spring, smells she had grown to greet like old friends.

There was the smell of the earth, a peaty, rough, and comforting smell. The smell of the grass, a sharp, green smell of growing things. The delicious scent of wild flowers beginning to bloom. The clean smell of the wind as it rustled the green leaves that garlanded the head of the giant tree.

A cow lowed, and a lamb answered with a long bleat of joy. Joan's heart raced with happiness. To celebrate one's Feast Day on such a day as this was to be happy twice over.

Their soup was waiting for them. They ate it with large, wooden spoons and then tipped up the bowls and licked the wood clean. Everyone had his own bowl. Joan's had a large J chiseled into the rim. Hauviette had the guest bowl, always washed out carefully after each use.

Joan giggled. She couldn't help herself. She knew her friend was waiting for some Feast Day sign. And, so far, it had been only a typical morning.

Madame d'Arc said, "Joan?"

"Yes, Mother."

"Go to the church, now. It is time for Mass. Then come back. You, too, Hauviette."

The two girls walked soberly in the sunshine toward the church. On the way, they passed the Enchanted Tree. The Enchanted Tree was so old and so enormous he was more than a tree. His huge, rough-barked trunk was eight feet across. He had hundreds of branches, some as big around as ordinary trees. When he burst into green, each spring, he looked like a gigantic umbrella, spreading his shade for hundreds of feet, standing up straight and tall under the clear, warm sun.

All the village people knew the fairies who lived in the trunk and the branches of the Enchanted Tree had to be treated

with respect. So the girls walked around
the tree counterclockwise, as children in
Domrémy had for generations, and then
they curtsied to the trunk and each one
made the sign of the cross on his chest
with his right index finger. Then they ran
off at top speed to the church. Though it
was small and modest, much thought and love
had gone into its building.

Father Perrault, the village priest, was an
old man of fifty. (People did not live as long
in those days as we do today.) His white hair
was cut in the shape of a bowl. His face was
smooth and pink, except when he was saying
Mass. Then it wrinkled up a little, and grew
serious.

Early-morning Mass was never well at-
tended. There was too much to do at that
hour. Father Perrault whispered and mumbled his way through the responses as fast
as he could. He had other duties in mind.

The church on this fine spring morning
was cold. But Joan, kneeling on the stone
floor, did not feel uncomfortable. In fact,
she felt as though she were floating. She had
always liked both Mass and Father Perrault.
Today, her feeling was stronger than liking —

and stranger, too. It was mixed up somehow with her Feast Day. With something that had awakened with her that morning. Something wonderful was to happen. She felt she would receive presents bigger and more splendid than she could imagine.

She lifted her head to look for a moment at the face of the archangel. The sun was almost directly behind the stained-glass window — the people of Domrémy had worked many months to create it — and she blinked at his glory.

The Archangel Michael, his wings folded behind him, looked down upon the pews. He held a scroll in his hand, upon which were written the Ten Commandments. There was a gold circle of light above his head sparkling with precious stones. Today, he seemed to be made of colored fire. It was difficult to look him in the face — he was so bright and beautiful.

Quite naturally, as though it were a normal and friendly thing to do, Archangel Michael smiled at her.

She was looking directly at him, and there was no mistake. Michael, with his white wings half-folded behind him, looked at her and

stretched his mouth in a wide, kind smile. Joan blinked and looked away. When she looked back he was still smiling. Then she closed her eyes, and when she opened them again, Michael was as he had always been; he no longer smiled.

But he had; he had smiled at her with a smile of promise.

Outside the church, her feet were winged. She felt as though she could fly. She felt as though the smile of the great angel had been part of her Feast Day. And it was just beginning, this extraordinary day. Just beginning.

Joan was one of the fastest runners in the village. She raced back to her house. When she entered she stopped and gave a small gasp.

Her Feast Day present was there, lying on the wooden dowry chest. It was a mirror, a polished sheet of bronze, scoured and scoured again patiently with sand until it gleamed. It was roughly a half foot in diameter, and it was round. It was girded by an oak frame. The frame was what her brother had been making. Joan stood in awe. A mirror of her own! Not even her mother had such a thing. Only great ladies used mirrors. As she stood still, not believing, her mother said behind her, "It's yours, Joan. Pick it up and look. For a happy Feast Day."

Her face stared back at her out of the shimmering metal. It was the face of a little girl, and she thought for one odd moment that it wasn't her face at all, but someone else's. Then she smiled, and her reflection smiled with her. She noticed her hair was mussed from her running, and she rearranged it with her fingers. Her reflection did the same.

It was all beyond her dreams.

She turned, holding the mirror, and rushed into her mother's arms. She didn't know whether to laugh or cry. She was so happy she did a little of both.

"Upstairs, now," Isabelle said. "Tidy up your room."

Holding her present to her, Joan climbed the ladder to her small room, where she plumped out the sacking she slept on. She used a broom that was nothing more than a bundle of hay bound to a tree branch. The broom made a rustling sound as she swept the floor, raising dust that settled again — though, after all, in different places. When she was through, the room looked neat and snug, like a friendly dog that has just been groomed.

When she came down again there was the smell of fresh bread in the air. Her mother made the round, flat loaves in a stone oven which stood open to the air in the back of the house. Usually, she baked only once a week, on Saturdays. But today was a weekday, and yet there was the hot sweetness of baking bread. And there, on the chest, golden brown and crusty and warm, was a round, mouth-watering loaf.

Joan went over to the loaf and poked it with an experimental finger. She still carried

her mirror clutched in her other hand. The loaf was not quite ready to eat. She was hungry.

Isabelle bustled in from outside and stopped, smiling at her daughter. Joan's mother had a sharp, hard, drawn face, with black eyes much like Joan's, and two parallel creases running down the sides of her cheeks. But when she smiled, her eyes became kind, full of somber laughter. They made Joan imagine what her mother had looked like at eighteen. She had been told often enough what a beauty Isabelle had been. Even her father, his round face lined with the worry of his responsibilities, would smile when he spoke of his bride of twenty years ago. And Joan could see, especially at those times, why her parents had loved, married, and lived together all these years, even though life was not easy and they had to work from sunrise to sunset just to keep enough food in their bellies.

"It's not baking day," Joan said, as though to herself.

Isabelle coughed dryly. "We have visitors coming," she said. Her eyes twinkled in spite of themselves as she watched her daughter.

Joan said eagerly, "Visitors?"

"Yes. Your uncle and your godfather."

Uncle Lassois was a happy-go-lucky sort of man, who neglected his business (he was a farmer) and often, too often, had to borrow money. He borrowed from Jacques d'Arc as he did from all his relatives and friends—small sums that were rarely paid back. They were too insignificant to cause a real break between the brothers. And besides, Lassois was a valuable friend in other ways. When he wasn't feeling low and out-of-sorts he was a jolly enough fellow and always full of news. He was interested in the world outside Domrémy, and that was a rare thing, indeed, for a peasant. Lassois came from a town a few miles away, Burey-le-Petit, and always brought news of the war. He was a sort of living newspaper, and his friends grudged him neither food nor drink.

As for the war, it had begun before Joan's father had been born. He, and Joan in her turn, had grown up with it. It wasn't a long, continuous war, but rather, a series of small wars between England and France.

It had lasted so long that some Frenchmen

had come over to the English side. They called themselves "Burgundians" after their lord, the Duke of Burgundy, who was in England's pay. Their hope was to subdue all France and turn it into an extension of England. Joan's village, Domrémy, built on the river Meuse, was loyally, fiercely, pro-French. On the other side of the river was another village, Maxey, which was Burgundian. Little love was lost between the two.

In their tiny way, the two villages of Domrémy and Maxey constantly rehearsed the great war, which was fought, time without end, beyond the limits of their small lives. There were constant battles between the boys of Maxey and the boys of Domrémy. And not only boys! The girls, too, would join the fight. It was playing and yet it wasn't. The fights frightened Joan, but she often joined in. She was one of the best stone throwers in Domrémy, though she had a habit of bursting into tears whenever her stones found their mark.

Joan was big for her age. She could spin better than most of the women in the village by the time she was ten. But what she loved best was to tend sheep. Especially, of course, in the spring and summer. Today, this bursting, brilliant day in May, she longed to be out in the fields. Some of the sunlight seemed trapped behind her black eyes. There was a small spark imprisoned there, dancing and leaping.

"Go on," Isabelle said. "It's your Feast Day. Go on out to the fields, Jeannette. Be home in time. Everyone is coming mostly because of you. So don't be late."

"Can I take my mirror?"

"No. Leave it. It will be here when you get back."

"All right," Joan said. She stepped out into the sunlight.

On a sloping hill, overlooking Jacques d'Arc's house, lay the Bois Chenu. Joan hurried toward this forest, running across the meadow, leaving her footprints on the tender spring earth.

She stopped again by the side of the Enchanted Tree. A group of boys and girls gathered under its shade. They played games. They garlanded the tree. As Joan hesitated, Hauviette hurried to her and called, "Joan, come on. We're going to put up more garlands. For the spring."

But Joan shook her head and hurried on. She ran across the pasture and into the dark of the Bois Chenu. She followed an ill-defined brambled path. From time to time, she stopped and broke a twig or a young limb lying across her path. Her face was serious in the shadows. Her thoughts were like minnows in a pond, darting here and there, unreachable, ungraspable. Her Feast Day was not over. Something was going to happen. Something . . .

Deep in the forest, up the side of a wooded hill, there was a waterfall. Near the rushing stream, ice-cold and clear in summer, moving under a thin blue sweater of ice in the winter, a niche had been hollowed out. It had been carved out of the wood of a chestnut tree. The hollow had been painted and gilded, and Joan's favorite saint, Notre Dame de Bermont, represented by a painted statuette, filled the niche.

She had been somewhat clumsily, but lovingly, made by an unknown pious artist. She seemed to gaze with painted satisfaction upon the running stream. Above her head there hung a wooden crucifix.

Joan knelt before her and prayed. The sun

blazed down on her head. She prayed for
what had to happen to happen. She was so
full of her excitement, her anticipation, that
she lost all sense of time. When she rose, her
knees were stiff.

She knew that she would live through,
now, one of her "quiet" times, times when
she would not want to talk to anyone. This
feeling of having to be by herself had in-
creased in the past year. Normally, she was
a fun-loving girl. She liked to talk and run
and play with her friends. But when she felt,
as now, empty, lonely, expectant, she would
keep to herself. The feeling did not usually
last long. While it did, it was like looking out
the window on a Saturday morning and seeing
the rain sheeting down, and knowing you
could not play that day.

Back at the pasture, she followed her

sheep from place to place. There were a couple of hundred of them, all branded so that the owners could tell which belonged to whom. Her father owned some two dozen. Joan could tell the members of her flock from the others without looking for the brand. Over the years, they had become more than animals. They were her friends. Each and every ewe and ram had a personality. She was particularly fond of the bellwether. He had a small bronze bell tied about his throat with a piece of string, so that when he moved all the sheep followed after him — full of confidence that their leader would find them ever greener grass and more luscious pasturage.

The sheep stopped drifting after a while, and Joan sat down on a grassy mound. It was the middle of the afternoon. The sun still burned out of a deep blue sky, but its warmth was less intense. Joan threw herself on the grass and closed her eyes. Even through the skin of her eyelids she could sense the diffused gold, feel warmth on her skin. She wiggled her toes and sighed.

A voice said, "Joan, go home."

She nodded, without opening her eyes.

It had sounded like little Michel, the small
son of one of her neighbors.
The voice said again, "Joan, you had
better go home now. Your mother wants
you."
She rose and turned. There was no one
there. Michel must have run away. He was
only six and very shy. She began to walk
back to her house, first making sure that
the bellwether was tied to a tree stump by a
long cord which she had plaited out of grass.
He would not move, and the sheep would
stay with him. When she reached her house,
she could hear her mother moving about
inside. Joan pushed open the door. Isabelle
was setting out the last of her bread — a
dozen round, golden loaves, the last three
still steaming from the oven.
"You wanted me, Mother?"
Isabelle looked up in surprise. "Why, no.
I didn't send for you. Who told you I
wanted you, Jeannette?"
"I thought it was Michel. But there was
no one when I turned around."
"You left the bellwether tied up?"
Joan nodded.
"If you want," her mother said, "you can

have a slice of bread. I have some mending to do."

But Joan wasn't hungry now. She wandered into the small garden back of the house and sat down on the grass.

She noticed the light.

She was aware that the grass in front of her was changing color. The green was deepening. The garden was coming alive. The small wild roses that grew there, irregularly, seemed to deepen in their crimson.

As the light grew, Joan threw herself on her knees. She was not so much afraid as bewildered. She did not know what to do, whether to pray or just kneel. She made herself quiet and small inside. The light changed to a green-gold. Perhaps, Joan thought, she was ill. Perhaps there was something the matter with her stomach.

The bells of the church sounded out the hour.

She lifted her face. It was difficult to do. A hand seemed to press the back of her head, bending it down. Her head was so heavy . . . but she lifted it, stubbornly, her eyes blinking against the light, and she saw . . .

She saw a cloud from which there poured

forth a light. It flowed along her body, caressing every inch of her skin. It was almost tangible. It touched her, kindly and softly. Then the church bells stopped, and as the last silvery note died, a voice spoke.

It was high and clear. It spoke very slowly, in the French idiom of Domrémy, the same peasant French that Joan had spoken all her life. The high clear voice seemed to drive its message, syllable by syllable, through her thin dress and onto her bare skin. She would not have been surprised to have found the voice's words written on her afterwards.

Yet, for all its force and clarity, the voice was gentle, almost humble. It spoke quietly. What it said was not frightening.

The voice told Joan she must be a good girl. It repeated this several times, slowly. Joan bowed her head. It was difficult to be good—in the way she thought the voice meant. Yet, if that was what was wanted, she would have to try. Then the voice told her that God would help her. It changed its tone and grew silvery, like the Domrémy church bells, like the halloo of a hunting horn in the distance.

"You have been chosen," it said, again and again. "You are the chosen one."

Joan wondered what she had been chosen for. As though the voice could hear her thoughts, it answered her question. It told her that she must come to the help of the future King of France, the young Dauphin. "You will advise him," the voice told her, "in the name of God. He will listen to you. You will save France."

There were questions Joan would have liked to ask. How could she, still a young girl, help to save her country? Women — and she was not yet even a woman — did not go to war. Or advise kings. Not even noble ladies. She was only a peasant and the daughter of a peasant.

The voice ignored the doubts in her mind, though it said nothing in direct reply. It came to Joan that her questions would some-day be answered. There was time, much time still.

Quite quickly Joan grew used to the fact that all she had to do was to ask a question in her mind, and the voice would answer — when it wanted to. She asked, Who are you? The voice was silent.

She asked, When will you come to me again? The voice replied, "Soon." Then it added a warning. Saint Catherine and Saint Margaret would presently appear to her. She must do what they told her to do. They would be sent directly from God. Joan would know this by certain signs they would give to her.

Light played on her face. Out of the light there now flowed down upon her such love and tenderness that she almost drowned beneath its sweet rushing. She was filled with a joy she had never known before. It was not like the joy of running and playing; not even the joy of giggling and sharing secrets with Hauviette; nor the joy of owning her own mirror, which had been the greatest joy of all until now. But a joy that was beyond all these things, that was almost beyond joy itself. It was partly a sad feeling, partly thoughtful, partly sweet and partly bitter. It was . . . it was . . . Oh, she didn't know what it was, and she didn't care. It was enough that it was.

She never knew how long the feeling lasted. Slowly—because the voice knew how unbearable it would have been to Joan if it had gone quickly—the light faded, the voice fell silent, bliss was tenderly, compassionately withdrawn. She tried to keep the happiness. She lifted her arms to the sky, she sobbed out loud, "Take me with you! Oh, please, take me with you."

But, in the end, she was left alone. She felt her eyes tear, as though they had looked upon the sun too long. She was so lost in her miserable happiness, she hardly looked up when the yelling began in the street beyond her house.

It grew louder. She could make out excited voices without hearing words. Pierre came panting around the side of the house. His usually pale face, with its snub nose, was as red as his carrot-colored hair.

He yelled, "Joan, those fools from Maxey are at it again! We'll give it to them this time." He turned and rushed away, yelling back over his shoulder, "If you want to come along, hurry. It's going to be a good fight."

Joan walked around the side of her house to screams and dust. She bent down and found two stones as big as her fists. For some reason, most of the loose, small stones were concentrated in Domrémy. This gave it a considerable edge over its stone-poor opponents of the village of Maxey.

Swinging her weighted arms, Joan half-ran toward the scene of the fighting. They were battling near the Bois Chenu. She could see some fifteen or twenty gesticulating forms. She tried to catch a glimpse of her brother's carrot-top in the fight, but the boys and girls were still too far away.

She began to run across the field.

Halfway to the fighting, she slowed. Then she stood, the stones still caught in her fists, listening. With a sob of gratitude, she went down on her knees. The sounds of the miniature battle grew clearer, then smaller, and faded away. The grass was again green-gold. The rosy light poured down.

The voice was clearer than it had been before. It spoke more rapidly, as though it had grown more used to Joan. It told her all over again to be a good girl (which seemed rather silly since so little time had passed). It told her, again, that she was to save France. And it added, within a few years. But miniature battles were not for her. She had real ones to prepare for. The voice called her "Child of God." Then, again reading her

secret mind, the voice granted her dearest wish.

A golden cloud above her parted. She saw briefly a miraculous blue—the blue of dreams, the blue of a summer sky as you remember it in winter. Then, through the slit, two small feet appeared. They were naked and innocent, the soles pink as if they had been rouged, the toes and toenails like those of a baby, only larger. The legs followed, and then the whole figure.

It was not large—maybe three feet high. It seemed to shimmer in the air, as though fighting an invisible wind. Joan looked past the manly shoulders and into the face, strong and calm. The wings were there. She caught her breath in ecstasy. Sweeping out from the shoulders, unfolded, they formed the shape of a cross, with the wings as the arms and the body as an upright.

She knew it was truly Saint Michael. His hands made the sign of the cross. There were trails of gold light where his fingers moved. With her fists still clenched around the stones, Joan followed the figure's movements, imitating them as she knelt on the spring grass.

She did not know how much time had passed, but after a while, the vision retreated into its glory, the feet still joined together, the face calm. The great eyes, of a color she could never remember, looking lovingly at her. The Saint retreated until he was enfolded in light. Then he was gone.

She looked numbly at the stones in her hands—and dropped them. The Saint had told her many things. She must see the priest, Father Perrault, and tell him of her vision. Joan was certain she had been part of a miracle.

She was halfway to the church before she noticed that both her hands were bleeding. In her ecstasy, she had clutched the stones too tightly.

Father Perrault sat in his dark, little room, at the rear of the church, and thought about his dinner. It was as insufficient, as uncertain, as everything else in his life. The parish of Domrémy was desperately poor. Periodically, the enemy, the Burgundian French, descended upon the village and despoiled it. On one occasion his church, the wonder of Domrémy, had been set afire. He had managed to put out the flames before they did any real damage.

Today, he was full of sad memories. Tonight, there would be no meat, no fowl for his table. He would have to eat last summer's vegetables, still smelling of the damp, earthy cellar in which they had been preserved.

The knock on the door startled him. He hitched his chair close to the battered table and called, "Come in."

Joan closed the small door behind her. The priest lit a candle. He was on good terms with the d'Arc family. He and Jacques were old friends. Joan's father had often helped him when help meant the difference between an empty stomach and a full one. He respected Isabelle d'Arc, though her harsh, intense face frightened him a little. Father Perrault, like most kindly men, disliked anyone who was not as simple as he. He was fond of children, therefore, and they of him. He made God lovable, kindly, and uncomplicated, like himself. He liked Joan, although, privately, he thought her too serious for her age. For a moment, he wondered why she had come to visit him in his little room back of the church.

"Sit down, Jeannette. I haven't seen you in some time." He had already forgotten morning Mass.

Joan said nothing. There was truly no place to sit, except on the table, for Father Perrault had only one chair and he was sitting in it. The old priest frowned. His forehead was not used to wrinkles, and it soon relaxed into its usual, pink smoothness. Then he said, "Of course. Today's your Feast Day, isn't it?"

Joan nodded. "I got a mirror. As a present."

Father Perrault made the sign of the cross. "A real mirror?" he asked. He was as incredulous and as impressed with the gift as Joan. In his life, he had never seen a mirror. When he shaved, after honing his knife, he

looked at himself in the water of the well.
Often he cut himself as he did so.

"Yes, Father. My brother Jean made a
frame for it, out of wood."

"Well." Perhaps he should say something
about vanity, the old man thought. But it
seemed a shame to spoil the pleasure in
Joan's eyes. He invited her to sit on the edge
of the table and drew his cowl about his
head. This was his signal for Joan to begin
her confession. Half an hour later, Father
Perrault leaned back in his chair. He cleared
his throat. It wasn't that miracles didn't
happen. Thousands of them had happened.
He knew some of them by heart. But they
weren't supposed to happen here, in
Domrémy. And not to a little girl he had
himself christened.

He thought, I might as well ask some
questions. Perhaps Joan was romancing. At
this time there were many young people who
thought they were inspired by God. Father
Perrault remembered, with a shiver, the
Children's Crusades, some two hundred–
odd years before. The boy who had led the
children to the edge of the sea had also had
visions. He had gathered thousands of chil-

dren around him. Then, they had set off on a three-hundred-mile journey, without proper clothes or food. Hundreds had died of starvation and thirst because of one boy's conviction that he was God-inspired. He had been a little older than Joan, but not by much. Miracles were dangerous things. If Joan insisted, he would have to report her vision to the Bishop. That would start a train of events whose end he could not foretell.

"This angel," the old priest said, "what did he look like?"

"Like an angel, Father."

"Was he clothed?"

"Do you think the Lord has nothing to clothe him with?"

It was an impertinent reply, though delivered in a modest and submissive tone. The priest could find nothing to answer it with, so he decided to ignore it.

"How was he clothed?"

"As an angel, Father."

"Did he have hair?"

"I am not allowed to speak of that." Joan was as surprised as Father Perrault by some of her answers. It was as though someone had taken over her tongue and was speaking through her. She had no power over what she was saying.

"I see. Was he crowned?"

"He was very richly crowned. God has allowed me to tell you that."

Father Perrault was perplexed. He tried to remember what he had been taught in his early training for the priesthood. But his memory failed him. He had been too busy baptizing babies, hearing confessions, easing deathbeds, and celebrating Mass, too busy growing enough food to keep himself alive. He had dealt, perhaps too long, with simple things.

Joan's answers were not simple. He did remember that, except to saints, revelations direct from God were impossible. Otherwise, there would be no need for a church on earth. He was the interpreter of God's will, he and thousands upon thousands like him — priests, bishops and archbishops and cardinals, all the way up to the Pope, the Vicar of Christ. They were all interpreters.

It was possible that Joan was committing blasphemy. If so, he knew, looking at her, that she was completely unaware of it. He could not believe her, yet, deep within him, he felt a small doubt. He was most upset.

"How did you feel, my child, when, as you say, Saint Michael left you?"

"I wept," Joan said, slowly, "and I wished he could have taken my soul with him into heaven."

"And you were not frightened?"

"I was only sorry that he left me so soon. I shall always be unhappy when he leaves me."

Father Perrault pushed the candle forward in the dark little room. He studied Joan's face

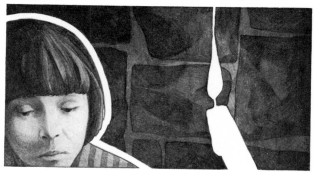

by its light. He could see nothing unusual. The child looked pale and tired. His heart went out in pity and concern for her. Maybe, he thought, she was possessed by a devil.

"Was he naked, your angel?"

"He was not," Joan said, loudly. "I have told you once before." She was not full of pride. She was, instead, full of the truth. There could be no doubt of it. She believed, irrevocably, in what she was telling him.

This was a subtle devil, Father Perrault thought, if indeed it was a devil. His tone sharpened and became slightly contemptuous. "Do they hate the English, your saints?"

"They love those whom God loves," Joan said, "and hate those whom God hates."

The priest coughed again. He said, "All right, Jeannette. You have seen a vision. I suggest you return to your home and forget about it. I will talk to your father tonight."

Joan's eyes widened. "But this is a secret, Father. I told you all this under the seal of the confessional."

"Your statements are a trifle . . ." Father Perrault paused, working his lips in and out as though he were sucking an orange. "I think, considering your age, I'd better talk to your father. You must not be encouraged to say these things. They could be dangerous."

What Father Perrault was thinking of was a terrible word—heresy. In this time, Catholics who brought down upon themselves the anger of the Church could end up in jail or even worse.

Joan said, earnestly, "You will not be able to, Father. Saint Michael told me. He has placed a seal upon your lips, as on mine. I cannot talk of these things to anyone. You are the only one I am allowed to talk with."

Father Perrault laughed.

"If that is so, then I shall not be able to tell him anything. We shall see." It was, he thought, the perfect test.

Joan frowned. "You will make a great fool of yourself, Father. God will not permit my secret to be told."

Father Perrault lost his temper, at last. He had had a trying time. Joan's calm replies, her assurance, he thought, hid only impertinence.

"Go home," he said, "and pray God to curb your tongue. He might have made you more respectful to your elders, instead of sending you visions. Now, go on."

"I'm sorry," Joan said, "I didn't mean to be rude." She stood, curtsied, and left. The door closed quietly behind her.

Father Perrault sat, thinking. The more he thought, the greater grew his uncertainty. He knew there was no real evil in little

Jeannette. She had an overactive imagination. But he would have to talk to Jacques, to explain to him that his daughter was having visions. Dangerous visions. Any revelation directly from God was a double-edged sword. The child could cut her life into pieces, without meaning to. She must be made to realize that some things are best left unsaid, some experiences best forgotten. Saint Michael was probably an undigested spoonful of soup or piece of meat.

There was no time to lose. Joan could be talking now to Hauviette, to any one of a dozen people who would soon decide she was mad or demon-possessed. In any case, he had to protect the girl against herself. The only person to whom he could go, the only one who had the authority to stop her, was her father.

The priest again put his cowl over his head and hurried out of his small room,

through the church itself, not pausing, hurrying with the small, mincing steps of the
elderly, hurrying to his old friend Jacques
d'Arc, hurrying to warn him of terrible
trouble that might still be prevented.

He was in such a hurry, he forgot to eat
his dinner. But then, that wasn't such a
shame. He had left behind him only a plate
of turnips and carrots. First things came first.
He felt that, if he were not saving a life, he
might well be saving a soul. That was more
important than a dinner, especially such a
dinner.

As Father Perrault's feet scuffed the dust
of the street, turning it to a gold haze in the
late afternoon sun, Jacques d'Arc lay on his
bed, sleeping. This was not usual for him. He
was an active, hard-working man. But he had
felt slightly ill after his lunch (which he took
out in the fields where he turned the earth
with his most prized possession—his ploughshare) and he had come home for a nap.

His ploughshare was his passion. He loved
it almost as much as he loved his family. He
had made it himself. It was an aristocrat of
ploughshares. No one in the village, no one,
he sometimes thought, in France, had any-

thing like it. But then, no one he knew had the secret of how to make such a tool except himself. He had kept his secret to himself all his years.

It had taken him thirteen months to find the stock alone — oak, a board of oak as flawless as a fine diamond. The grain of it had run straight as a ruled line, the wood was perfect and sound. He had bought the plank from the old carpenter Guibert, who lived in Vaucouleurs. He had haggled over the price of the wood.

Guibert had whistled through his teeth when he had shown Jacques the plank. "He's of good stock, he is," the carpenter said. "Yes, of good stock. I haven't seen a piece like him in two, three years."

Jacques, running his hand over the plank, lifting and feeling its weight, kept his face blank as stone. It would not do to let the carpenter know how he felt about the wood. It was the finest plank he had ever seen. He said, carelessly, "It's not bad. No knots. But underneath, who knows?"

"Don't take it then," the old man said. "I can use it. I'll make something fit for the Seigneur. You don't have to take it. It's expensive stock. Not for peasants. Look around, maybe you'll find something else." In the end, he bought the plank for ten sous, an enormous price for a piece of wood, wrapped it in sacking, and took it back to his house.

In the back garden of his home, Jacques dug a deep hole. He waited patiently until it filled with water. He put the plank in the hole and left it there to steep for three days and three nights. Then he took the wood and twisted it against his thigh until the soaked plank had taken on the shape he wanted. He took the bent wood, and nailed it to a rigid board, and let it dry for two weeks. When he freed it, it remembered its former shape, but only a little, just enough, and he had the exact curve he wanted. Then he shaped it, adzing the wood delicately with his iron hatchet, and the ploughshare became obstinate, sharp and arrogant. It had the hollow flank of an animal that has raced across hills, and a fine, smooth skin. Jacques could balance it on his fist.

When he showed it to Isabelle, he held the fine ploughshare against the light of his hearth fire. It shone there, bare as a knife.

"Oh," Isabelle said, her usually harsh

voice as soft with admiration as a young girl's. "That's lovely. It looks like the prow of a ship."

Jacques's pride in his work was daily renewed as the fine wood blade furrowed the earth and helped grow the food his family ate. The ploughshare was a constant source of satisfaction to him. He told no one where he had got the wood, or how he had made it. It seemed to him somehow wrong to do this, as though he were betraying a family secret.

Now, he lay asleep and dreaming in his big iron bed, asleep in the late afternoon. His stomach rumbled from time to time. He moved uneasily in his slumber, and beads of sweat pearled his round, red face. Once, he opened his mouth and groaned, "No, no," and turned and twisted.

The knock on the door was loud as thunder. It interrupted his dream and awakened him. He swung to the side of his bed and went to the door. His nightmare was still gathered about him like an invisible mist. He wasn't sure whether he was asleep or awake. His dream had been so real it had frightened him. Dreams were serious things. They were auguries of the future.

When Father Perrault stumbled in, panting, Jacques rubbed his sweaty forehead and bent his head in a gesture of respect.

"Father," he said, "what can I do for you?"

"What good fortune. You're here, at home."

"I had a sour stomach," Jacques said. He sat down on one of the stools and motioned the priest to another.

"You're out of breath, Father," he said.

"I ran. It was important, Monsieur Jacques. Very important that I tell you . . ." Father Perrault stopped, his mouth open.

"I'm glad you're here," Jacques said. Both men were listening to what they were thinking, rather than to each other. "I just had a most unusual dream."

"About Jeannette," the priest said.

"About my daughter, Joan," Jacques said.

They had spoken at the same time.

They both stopped and looked at each other.

"I had this dream," Jacques said, slowly. "It seemed to me that I was upon a hillside, near the Bois Chenu. I heard the thunder of a troop of armed men, and then, sweeping down upon me there appeared a huge army, many thousands of soldiers. At their head, I saw a small figure clad in armor and carrying a white banner."

Father Perrault opened his mouth again, but Jacques waved it closed, impatiently.

"As the figure grew close, it looked more and more familiar. Finally, it swept by me, and I recognized Joan. She was riding her horse like a man, full saddle. What do you think, Father?"

"Only a dream," he said. "The Church attaches no importance to dreams. Young girls don't run away to be soldiers. They don't lead armies. Joan is a good girl. Your wife has often told me she is one of the best spinstresses in the village. She will think of marriage in a few years."

Jacques nodded. He spoke suddenly, his face twisted into a mask of fear and unhappiness.

"If I thought such a thing could happen to my daughter, I'd drown her in the nearest stream and hold her head under the water myself. Such unnaturalness. Hell is full of those who have done much less."

"T-t-t-t-t-t." Father Perrault clicked his

tongue against the roof of his mouth. "Joan's a good girl." He paused. "I don't think you need to worry."

"Well," Jacques said, a bit impatiently, "what's on your mind, Father? I've lost too many hours with this stomach of mine."

There was a strange look on the old priest's face. He shook his head slowly. "I just wanted to say hello," he said finally. "I mean— No, that's all. I know I must have had a reason for coming here, but I've forgotten." He shook his head again and repeated weakly, "I've forgotten. It couldn't have been important." He rose and walked to the door. "Excuse me," he said, a little clumsily, "excuse me for disturbing you. I must be getting old."

He yanked at the door latch and left, walking with small, desperate steps, and muttering to himself as he walked.

When he got home, he tried once more to justify his sudden visit to his old friend, but though he was vaguely aware that he had forgotten something, something important, he couldn't for the life of him remember what it was. It seemed simpler to Father Perrault to stop worrying about his memory and his old age. He said grace and turned to the roast chicken on his plate and began to eat.

After a few seconds, he stopped and stared. He remembered the carrots and the turnips he had left cooling there when he had hurried off to Jacques d'Arc's house. But there had been no chicken. No plump, roast chicken. He knew it. And yet, there it was.

It was the juiciest, most perfectly cooked bird he had ever tasted. He mumbled a little more to himself and decided that some kind neighbor had brought him this surprise.

Later, when he tried to find out who had given him his supper that night, everyone denied, shamefacedly, bringing him a chicken. It was as though someone had wanted to make up to him for something—for something he had forgotten.

Jacques, meanwhile, went back to his ploughing. He had decided to send Father Perrault some bread from next week's baking and a dozen eggs from tomorrow's laying. It was plain the man needed food. Hunger was making him old and forgetful.

As he ploughed the rich earth with his beautiful ploughshare, he thought of his dream. He decided to ignore it, if he could.

Joan sat on a tree stump in the pasture, watching her flock as they browsed, and she dreamed too. Not so much of things but of shapes and colors drifting through her mind like emerald and crimson clouds.

Her Feast Day had turned out as she had hoped. Wonderful things had happened to her. More wonderful things would happen. She did not know where her angel would lead her, but it could only end in beauty and in glory. Of that she was sure.

She plucked a blade of grass and nibbled it. She looked for a moment at the sun and then leaped to her feet. It was time to go home. There was company for dinner. There would be talk of the war. This time she must

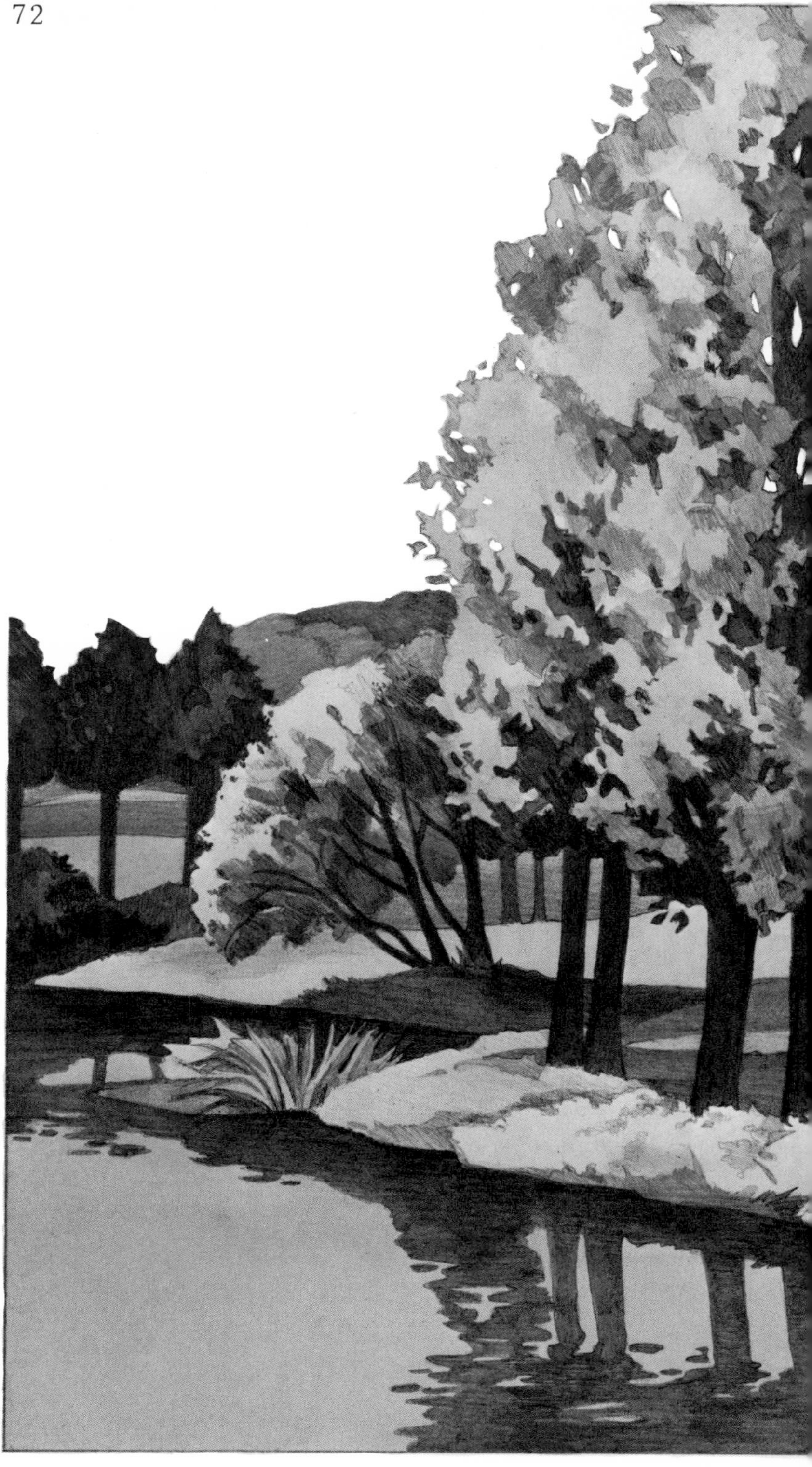

listen as she had never listened before. For they would be talking of her future profession, of what she must do. Not today, not tomorrow. But soon. It was time for her to begin to learn.

In time, her voices would come again, and with them her promised saints, lady angels, with whom she would talk almost informally. Something told her that Saint Margaret and Saint Catherine would be more approachable than the stern glory that was the Archangel Michael. In their time, they, too, had been young girls. They would understand the mixture of fear and ecstasy which filled her to overflowing.

She glanced down at the grass beneath her feet, somehow surprised that her happiness had not been spilled upon the ground for all to see — a rivulet of gold and crystal.

That night the d'Arcs and their guests — Jean Morel of Greux (one of Joan's godparents) and Durand Lassois — sat around the dinner table and talked after they had eaten. Durand had not brought his wife with him. At the last moment Madame Lassois had decided to remain at home, in Burey-le-Petit, nursing a spring cold.

The conversation turned, inevitably, to the war. The men spoke and drank deeply from their stone jugs of beer. They talked of their tortured country, sliced at from the outside by the English and from within by the Burgundian French. They talked softly. If they had not all been related, in one way or another, they would not have talked of such matters at all. As it was, their voices were hardly raised above a whisper.

The firelight gleamed and drove back the shadows. But the fire created only a half-light, and outside the little circle around the table, blackness thickened and menaced them from the closed door. Beyond, there was the still, dark, starlit sky.

"What's your opinion of all this, Morel?" Jacques took a sip of his beer. "Will we ever be free?"

Jean Morel shook his head. He was a tall, thin man with deep lines running horizontally along his forehead and down the sides of his face. They were deep enough to catch the shadows. In the flickering light, he looked as though he had been scratched by some wild animal. His nose was long and hooked. He worked as a dyer of woolens. His hands and nails were permanently stained by the colored juices of the press which he serviced day after day.

"The situation is more hopeless than ever. After all this time . . ." He sighed and others sighed with him. They remembered the long years of war. Years of gentle starvation and diminishing hopes. Years of slow, poisonous English occupation. Years of watching Frenchmen become Englishmen.

"Uncle Morel, do you think the Dauphin's mother will ever take him seriously?"

"I doubt it, Pierre. She's too busy with her own affairs to bother about the son she mothered so casually." Everyone knew that the Dauphin's mother was not the most virtuous of women.

Durand Lassois said softly, "They tell me she lets it be said that the Dauphin's a bastard."

Pierre's elder brother, Jean, said abruptly and bitterly, "If he isn't by birth, he is by reputation."

Joan bit her lips. They were talking about her King, the one she was going to help free, the one she would one day see anointed the true King of France. She thought of the

Dauphin as a little doll she could put in her pocket and take out, secretly at night, and mother.

Morel said, quietly, "He couldn't own his own country now if he wanted to. Even what is left after the possessions of the Duke of Burgundy"—his face settled even more deeply into its harsh lines as he pronounced the name of the most hated man in France—"even what is left is divided up among the barons. We'll never be free while the Dauphin plays croquet at Chinon and sells what's left of his country to the English, bit by bit, to pay his debts."

Then they talked of crops, of the scarcity of metal money, and the fact that all specie was different, so that a man might be wealthy in one part of France and a pauper in another. His money did not hold good, as it should, the length and breadth of the land.

But always, the talk came back to the war, the everlasting war.

Jean Morel leaned back in his stool, pushing it nearer the dying fire, and said, "Joan, you're a young woman—almost."

"Nonsense," Isabelle said, sharply. "She's only a child."

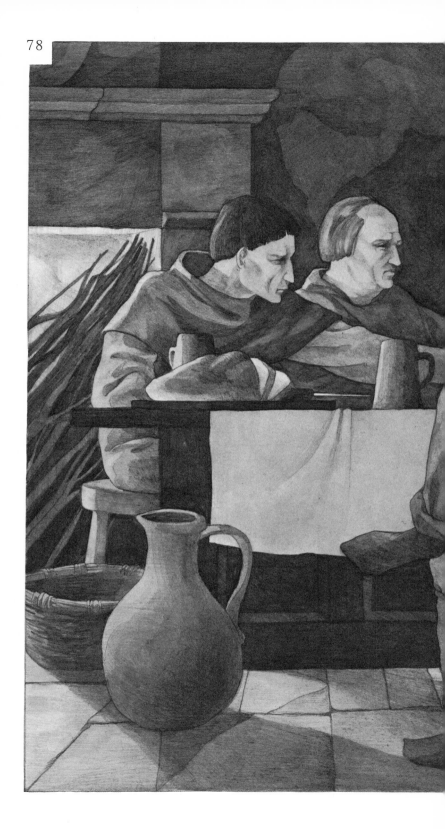

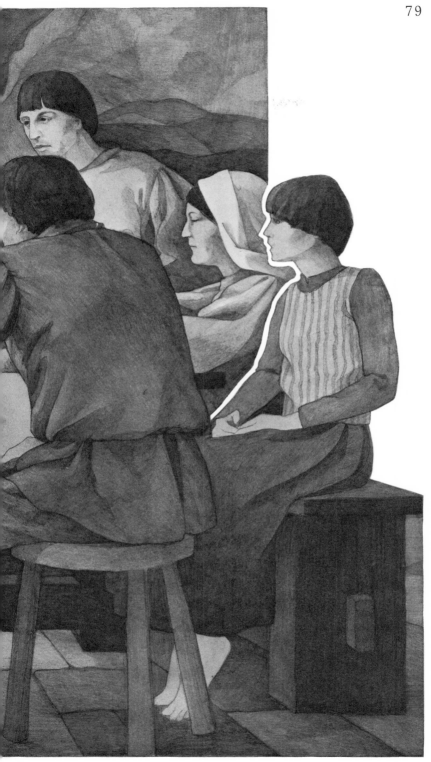

"Tell me," Joan's godfather continued, "where do your political sympathies lie?"

A gust of laughter swept the table. Joan said nothing. Isabelle nudged her with a sharp elbow. "Answer when you're spoken to."

Joan looked up, blushing. "With my gentle little Dauphin, of course," she said. "And he is not a bastard!"

Pierre said, "If we were truly men, we would take arms and fight. If there were any army to fight with. And the hell with the Dauphin. Let him play croquet till he rots."

"There is no army," Durand Lassois said, nervously. He disliked violence. "The country's broken into bits, into small fiefdoms."

Jacques asked, "Has anyone heard about a new English invasion? There've been rumors."

"I heard them, too," Lassois said. "They say Sir John Falstaff is on his way from England and a thousand men with him. We do nothing but wait."

"With a thousand Frenchmen," Joan heard herself saying, "we could sweep the English from France and send them back to their own land. With a leader, we could finish this war within one year." She was in tears inside. It

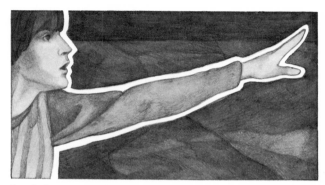

had happened again. Something had taken over her tongue, something was speaking through her. There was nothing she could do.

Jacques took a gulp of beer and looked at his daughter. "Joan," he said, "since when do you volunteer opinions on matters of war?" He took another drink. "I have had a dream. If what I dreamed were to come true, I repeat to you in front of your mother and our relatives what I told poor Father Perrault this afternoon." He looked at Joan's brothers. "If I believed the thing I have dreamed of her should come to pass, I should want you to drown her. And if you did not do so, I would drown her myself." His voice was heavy with fear and rage. The brothers looked silently and uncomfortably at each other. Their father's rage was inexplicable.

The two guests were embarrassed, staring into the embers of the fireplace. Joan burst into tears.

"All right," Isabelle said. "That's enough. It's her Feast Day, remember. I won't have her frightened by your rough talk. You make no sense. Lassois, Morel, I beg your pardon for my husband. He forgot himself. Jeannette, go to your room. It's been a long day."

Joan, still sniffling, rose to her feet. She kissed her mother and her godfather on the cheek, looked hesitatingly at her father's furious face, shook hands with her Uncle Lassois, and gave Jean a hug. She whispered in his ear, "Thanks for my present." Then she turned and left them there, silent, bewildered, thinking their different thoughts.

In her room, she climbed out of her dress. Then, instead of snuffing out the candle which she had taken from the main room to light her way to bed, she carefully put it on the narrow windowsill. She took out her Feast Day present from beneath her bed where she had put it. She unwrapped the mirror from its cloth protection. Finally, she lifted the candle up, and put it close to the bronze, and looked.

At first, wavering, indistinct, she saw her
face. Then, as though there were some other,
growing source of light — fiercer, by far, than
her feeble candle flame — her reflection became more distinct. But it was not her face.
The face of a woman gazed out at her. It was
stern and glorious, and there was light in the
black eyes. On her head there was a white
casque of war with a white plume. In the
background, she could see her hand. It
bore a sword. The sword was naked, and
flashed in the mysterious light.

For some seconds she looked at her face
as it would be many years from now. Then,
the candle was snuffed out, as if by some
mysterious finger and thumb.

She fell to her knees and prayed. She had
been given a sign, a testament. She knew her
future now. It would comfort her and sustain
her during her waiting in the years to come.
It was the greatest sign she had ever been
given. It was a sign of victory. Beyond that,
all was dark.

As her Feast Day faded, Joan knelt by the
side of the pile of sacking on which she slept.
She crossed herself in the dark and whispered, "May God bring me victory." Then,

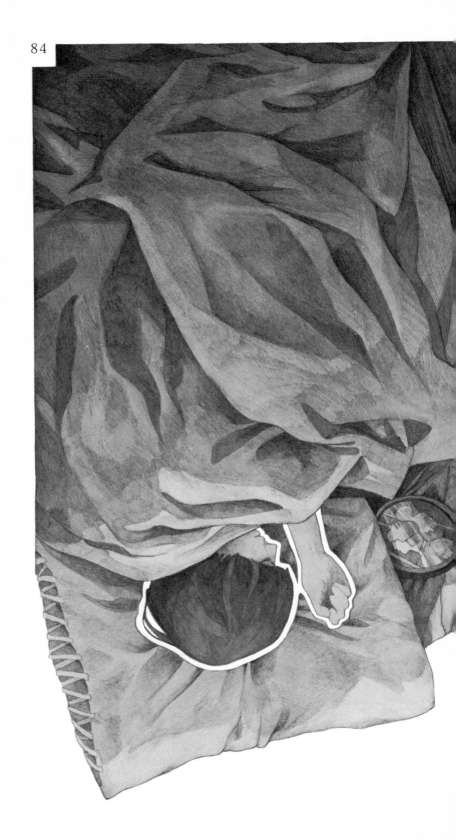

she lay down upon her rough bed and waited for sleep. She waited with the same calm with which she would wait for her destiny. Her Feast Day was over.

After a while, she fell asleep. In her sleep, she smiled.

THE BEGINNING

AFTERWORD

Joan's first visions were only the beginning: the beginning of a glorious, short, tragic life. Here, briefly, is what happened to her:

Around January 12, 1429 (three and a half years after the Feast Day that you have just finished reading about), Joan persuaded Robert de Baudricourt to send her to Chinon, where the Royal Court of France, headed by the Dauphin, was located. The Dauphin allowed her into his presence, hiding himself among the crowd of nobles and pages so that Joan, who had never seen him, might not recognize him. But she approached him without hesitation, and he talked to her privately for two hours. She told him that she was "God's messenger, sent to tell you that you are the true heir to France and the King's son."

At the head of a small army she relieved the siege of Orléans, a French town that was being attacked by the British. This was only the first in a series of victories which culminated in a march into Reims, where the Dauphin was crowned Charles VII, King of France.

Against Joan's advice, Charles VII signed a truce with the Burgundians which was to last until Easter of 1430.

Joan of Arc was captured, through a blunder, at Compiègne by the Burgundian French. The King made no attempt to ransom her. In truth, he was afraid of this young girl who in a short time had accomplished what the French had been unable to do for so long: to liberate and unify France. The Burgundian French, realizing her importance, sold her to the British. She was taken to the English

military center of Rouen, and there tried for heresy by English and Burgundian clergy. Her main prosecutor and worst enemy was a Burgundian bishop named Pierre Cauchon.

Joan was condemned by Cauchon as a heretic. She was tied to a stake in the Rouen marketplace on the morning of May 30, 1431, and was burned to death. She was nineteen years old.

Out of her agony she was to emerge crowned with sainthood. She was to become a symbol for France, and for the whole world, of bravery and truth. Her death, like the death of anyone who is good and beautiful, was not to be in vain. She remains an immortal in man's memory.

BIBLIOGRAPHY

Belloc, Hilaire. Joan of Arc. New York: McMullen, 1949.

Paine, A. Bigelow. Joan of Arc. New York: Macmillan, 1925.

Waldman, Milton. Joan of Arc. London: Longmans, Green, 1935.

You might want to read one of the greatest plays on Joan's life, written by George Bernard Shaw, and titled Saint Joan. You can also find in your public library a transcript of Joan's trial, titled The Trial of Joan of Arc.